SCHIZOPHRENIA IN TEENAGERS - FOR PARENTS AND TENAGERS II.I [A DIARY]

PUBLISHED BY : www.createspace.com

I0407861

I HOPE THIS JOURNAL HELPS OTHERS IDENTIFY SCHIZOPHRENIA IN THEIR LIVES – AT ANY TIME YOU CAN KEEP YOUR OWN DAY-TO-DAY "JOURNAL" – YOU DO NOT HAVE TO WRITE AN ENTRY EVERYDAY

YOU ARE NOT MEANT TO MEMORISE ANY OF THIS JUST READ IT AND TAKE IT IN AS IT COMES

PAUL ARMSTRONG

[1] 18/ 12 / 2016

I feel kind of lonely and depressed at night especially when it gets dark early. I find it hard to rest during the day when I want to. I think it helps to keep a journal of my feelings for each day. Writing my feelings down easy easier than any other way. I hope I can succeed in writing a journal which would help others. Its only when the hurt builds up to a certain level that I can feel a peace, a feeling of rest that comes from the heart. Most days this does not happen. I have very weak long term memory; in school I was a cramer. The best thing I experience is a good cry. You are going to have to ask the lord to give you that. I know that enjoying is the key to cure you in the long run but where I am now I am not able to enjoy for very long – I just get depressed if I do. One thing the medication does do in the long run is reduce daydreaming – They get worse and worse before you get help and are usually on a repetitive topic. Having a pet animal helps a lot because – they respond in a loving way to your attention. Once I left secondary school that is when my problems really began I couldn't cope with studying. Schizophrenia affects your level of intelligence but when I found the right medication AND took it consistently my intelligence increased. I lacked the ability to say NO to people and I never stood up for myself.

[2] 19/12/2016

I'm in my forties and life is just staring for me. I don't feel that life is over for me h like I did in my twenties and thirties. I know that in my teenage years I used to love staying up in the sitting room late at night with the light turned off – I would crouch in front of the fire and just soak up the heat. Going for walks in winter especially at night – helped me feel at peace. Nowadays I find that sitting on my bed with my eyes closed in silence for ten minutes - when I reopened eyes I would some peace and relief. Withdrawal is a part of schizophrenia not defending myself, taking less care of myself, wanting to stay in bed all morning and then staying awake late into the night etc. I did some crazy things in my teenagers [I'm not going to say what] Studies show that if people stay at home with their parents they are twice as likely to stick to their medication. I do have a type of autism – that means I am content being just with my family. I had a difficult relationship with my dad and turned more towards my mum – I am guessing this is the same with other schizophrenic people. I [In my adult life – thirties] started affirming my dad as a good man and that any advice he gave me was in my best interests – I kept doing this and now I have a really good relationship with my parents. A great thing I found and something that helped bringing out the emotions was when I would kneel on the floor my chest and head resting on the bed – I would press the palms of my hands over my eyes and stay there for a few minutes – I would feel a peace afterwards. To note : This only works best when you've been depressed. I would encourage parents to send their schizophrenic son, daughter to mental health activities such as

[in limerick] Inis Cara, Le Cheile or mensheds.ie . If teenagers are going to talk about their feelings it would be better to leave that to the professionals, those outside the family. AND a visit or email to the Samaritans is highly recommended. What I now realize is that qualities my parents had that they tried to pass on to me : getting up in the morning; keeping myself active / working for my dad; eating healthy foods and not trying to pass the time by eating junk food; that I should go to sleep at a certain time as a matter of discipline. I went through several episodes of not taking my medication and I have been in 5B [Psychiatric Unit] a few times. Parents if you find one activity that your children love doing – encourage them to do that activity every day. Some of the mistakes I made before I developed schizophrenia were continued because I had schizophrenia- such as an inability to commit to certain activities. With SZ I find it hard to rest until I am really tired. I had a really happy childhood and this has stood by me all my life. I have had a type of autism so when I went to college I was at sea with everyone fighting their corner to make and keep friends. I am finding that sitting in a dark room with just the light of the computers is very peaceful. SZ begins in teenagers just when young people learn to relate to the opposite sex and develop their social skills – I had a nervous breakdown and for many years I have been just slightly mad – this showed up especially in my college years when I should have learned to stand up for myself. I used to be afraid of girls but I did really like one particular girl and I was confident then. When I was in my 20s it seemed that this was my world forever and I would never recover from my sufferings. Now I am forty and my world is just beginning to start; I don't worry about what I cannot have: I am happy with who I am now. I suspect that a lot of people with SZ also have autism. A problem with SZ is difficulty in saying no to people: Bur schizophrenic people all [I think] have redeeming qualities for me it was being honest, being a forgivable person, being generous. Another problem is with SZ that I keep going back to things that do not make me happy – such as playing the same computer all the time: eating too much junk food and not looking after my health – I knew this was not good for my health but I kept doing it. Depression is like a pain as much as I try to cure myself straight away I know it will take time. My parents were patient with me – I am guessing this came from the doctors advice. At 40 I realize that not everything is learned in school. SZ's are not good at taking care of themselves this does change over time. Mentally ill patients often cite the argument of 'Side-Effects" me among them – but now knowing that I need it to cope and seeing the positive effects that taking medication consistently has had on me I am willing to stick with the medication. The one thing SZ people lack is love especially if they are living alone. One thing I have found is that hugging a pillow to your chest makes you feel better.

[3] 20 / 12 / 2016

Sometimes I feel I just cannot cope I am groaning inwardly. This feeling does not last long but it is very tough. People don't think about heaven; people want to live forever but after a long time of suffering you may long to go to heaven. Another problem I suffer is from hallucinations – pictures making faces at meh; shapes forming on the floor / walls and curtains etc. When you have experienced suffering for a long time without giving in – you get cranky. Someone once said that old people have a right to be cranky because they have so many ailments in their life. A cross I bear from SZ is not being able to memorize any real amount of information – So I struggled in secondary school but I have found things that I really enjoy doing that rely on creativity rather than memorizing. I am learning to make decisions and choose not to be afraid and to stick by my decisions whether right or wrong. What I have learned that in secondary school doing homework should be mixed up; part of one subject and then part of another subject. And to discipline myself and stop working after a certain time – my parents would often ask me to go to sleep something I did not do – I should have taken easier subjects so I could complete all of my homework each night

[4] 21/12/2016

In secondary school I got into the habit of playing music while doing my homework – i thought this would help me to concentrate but it only made learning harder for me – nevertheless I continued to do this. Depression is linked to low self-confidence and poor self-esteem. I had particular problems with girls. I was the nice shy pleasant student that girls: are all are attracted to. I was hating myself and could not commit to a relationship with a girl. I let other people have control over my life – The experience of being made responsible for everything was something I experienced a lot. I did not stand up for myself. I could not treat other people as bad – they did bad things to me and I should have asserted myself. Everyone makes mistakes in life – seeing other people live their lives in spite of a stigma I now know that past mistakes should not prevent you from having a full life. Even to be seen as enjoying myself. Other people are able to take care of themselves – if they stop fighting you, you can then stop fighting too. I have found that when it hurts – just talking aloud and saying something like " I am hurting / I am not strong enough " – each day I do this I feel a little bit better [God is real] I find that when I try to rest at times I am unable to – Persist here because the tension only lasts a few minutes. It is nearly night-time and I am feeling kind of lonely and depressed. There is a barrier to me feeling completely relaxed. My schizophrenia along with other problems have been with me for a long time I can't visualise the end of this is this wound going to heal. Can I be depressed and happy at the same time? Yes I am doing things I really enjoy but most evenings I still get depressed. It has taken great reassurance to believe that all suffering does end. I feel that there is something missing in my life. In the past I would just label it as depression. I can say I have led a full life though. I have a purpose in my life; I have learned a lot, suffered a lot; changed a lot; done a lot of good. If I had known in the past all the suffering I would endure I never would have coped. A salutary lesson to live in the present. What I have started doing recently is a willingness to try out things. Like asking for things. It is making me more confident. The mantra is "I can, I can, I can".

[5] 22/12/2016

I am in my 40s now and I am just learning to take care of myself mainly due to health problems which crop up as you get older. I find caring for myself helps with my self-esteem. Seeing yourself in a other person really helps – that's why reading a book like this is good for you. I find that when it is really tough it does not last long. I am starting to care for my health on a long-term basis and I have reduced my intake of junk foods and now take more vegetables and fruit. I am also getting more exercise and fresh air. I was unable in earlier years to eating healthy foods even though I knew it was not good for me – I would call this a form escapism. Right now I am feeling tired and restless at the same time. I am finding it hard to discern where sounds and voices are coming from. I am not an angry person in general it takes a lot of pressure to make me angry. I have to say that when I could have been most in danger; when I should have been most under pressure – I did not experience this – I felt strong because the lord carried me. When it comes to the heart it speaks to other person – So write your own journal at a time when you really want to. What I really want to say right now is that I am not afraid; I know I am suffering and I have plenty of enemies – but I have suffered for so long that I am stronger

[6] 24/12/2016

I am feeling kind of stressed right now. I am doing good but missing something. I would say this missing feeling is for God. Depressed people are more sensitive to the darkness in the world. But you know what suffering can make you beautiful. I have experienced this many times. I am fulfilled at the same time as depressed. I would say this is a cross I accept – it is not forever – medications and counselling treatments are getting better. You have to say that you will stick to the medication – your parents worry a lot – they see clearly how depression is affecting you whereas you do not. It is a sign that you are getting better when you accept you need the medication. Take it like you take food. I am doing the right things but it seems I am still suffering – things are getting better but slowly.

[7] 28/12/2016

I want to be happy before my suffering ends – I have been suffering for a long time now. Because of my suffering my faith has slowly strengthened. Basically I am doing the right things but I am still suffering – Groan! I strongly advise that you find a cause/purpose in life it will boost your self-esteem. I have found happy moments in my life. I think there is a dark side that fears change. I feel lonely at the moment. Socialising in third level college and afterwards was not my strong point. I kept running away from life. There are mountains of books on self-help but none of them worked. You can write your own journal if you like instead.

[8] 29/12/2016

I feel a little alone and depressed right now. If you have heard the story in the bible of Job you will have to trust that there is a happy ending. Crying is a big help for me when I am depressed. I feel the need to be alone that I am crowded out. I can't handle lots of noise it just makes me more depressed.

[9] 1/01/2017

God Cannot give you a happiness apart from himself – It simply is not there [C.S. Lewis] I am becoming less discouraged these days because I know if things go wrong this is not the final word in my life. At the moment I am feeling happy I have got to the stage where I can say I do not miss the things I do not have. I think our parents are the last generation that had this attitude. Maybe it is better to suffer if it redeems us.

[10] 2/01/2017

What I have learned is when you are most suffering the best approach is to sleep through it. It does get easier over time. I can't say how much important it is to stick with medication. People talk about side effects the reality is that this feeling is part of your sickness. I have seen both sides because I have lived so long with the illness. I am in my forties and now I take medication just like I eat food. It is a good sign you are getting better but yeah medication is long term. During my young adulthood I was terrified of girls I did not have much self-esteem. You need to be assertive – part of the illness is that I didn't say get lost Early on enough. I never stood up for myself – some people walked all over me. Part of my confidence was when I had the **courage** to fight my problems to believe that to fight would make me feel good about myself and it did / does.

[11] 3/01/2017

Have you ever come to the point where you just couldn't cope
– I have – that is when the love of another person really helps.
If you are writing your own journal it does not a!ways need to
be long.

[12] 4/01/2017

Today I conquered a barrier in my life with help. I am still
suffering in life which can be tough at times. If you are beyond
coping you need to ask for help. I do not know how I would
cope without family. As much as I like being on my own – I still
need love. I am not strong when it comes to physical suffering.
I personally think that S.Z.'s go through a lot of suffering but I
reckon if you stick To the meds it does have a happy ending.
My experience with S.Z. is that I wasted money on unhealthy
foods / magazines etc. Dad and mum would insist that I learn
to save money. I did not do so. It is very easy to spend money
when you have it.

[13] 5/01/2017

I keep going back to things that do not make me happy – like
computer coding or the same computer game. I am learning to
be true to myself – Even if what I like doing is boring to most

people – This is one part of making one happy. I am tired of suffering it has gone on for so long – So right now I feel a little depressed.

[14] 6/01/2017

I have learned to try out new things all the time. My sister once said "I'll try anything once" – it certainly boosts the self-esteem. I am constantly talking to the Lord it makes me less lonely. I am autistic so I don't mind being alone but I still need company every so o5ften. There are plenty of people who have autism and it is undiagnosed in them. Overall I think things are getting better. Someone told me once that hugging a pillow to my chest for a few minutes would make me feel better and it does. I have learned to cry all my suffering to God to tell him every so often that I just can't cope.

[15] 7/01/2017

I am feeling better now today but it is evening and I am feeling q little tired and run-down. Fighting sin which makes you happier is also tough. You can cash in your suffering for requests / rewards if you have suffered for a long time - I have. There is a latent feeling good about yourself if you have fought for a long time it is this way with me. Can you have good self-esteem and suffer at the same time YES. I feel the need to be alone right now [Nighttime]. My favourite room to be in is the kitchen on my own.

[16] 8/01/2017

I find that it is in the evening that I usually get depressed. I am autistic but schizophrenia really messed that up. I have found some good purposes in life; things that I did not learn in school. Right now I feel the need to be alone and just writing. Schizophrenic people are very brave but for me an inability to socialise meant I suffered A LOT. Someone did something bad to me and I would not fight I realise now that the best way to defend yourself is to be confident. Your suffering will not end over night but it does get better. A little hint if you want to keep your own journal – writing is all about removing what does not fit in to the letter.

[17] 9/01/2017

This morning I Felt that I just could not cope but this quickly passed. I did something new today and enjoyed it. Many a time in the past when I would try to enjoy myself I would get even more depressed than I usually do. I still find myself getting restless at times – being restless is a part of schizophrenia. The stairs is where I feel most relaxed; also I find that sitting on a cold surface such as the floor relaxes me BUT only in the evenings. I turned on the radio while writing this a habit I had when I was most ill with schizophrenia [Working And Listening At The Same Time] I used to keep doing this even though it did not make me happy and slowed my work down. I was unhappy in secondary school but did not realise this – I was struggling to keep up and was working late hours.

[18] 11/01/2017

When I am most depressed and tired that is when all my negativities and crankiness come out. I am feeling happy and not depressed right now. I am chilling out and enjoying myself. It has been a long time since I have felt this way. I have changed over the years – taking care of myself, eating healthier food, accepting my medication etc. For me life begins at 40.

[19] 12/01/2017

Today was a good day - Just to show you suffering does end. Three things make me happy a PROACTIVE relationship with God; a purpose in life; and parents. Parents are great and everyone I say this to agrees. I am lucky that I am in a HSE community residence with other people – I pay a small rent. It is good to be around other people with staff present to make sure I take care of myself; that I take all my medication; go to sleep at the right time and eat properly – The nursing staff are able to do this much better than parents would ever be able to.

[20] 13/01/2017

Once again have found that I just could not cope. I realise that I am pretty average without the help of others and I have received lots of help. From my own experience – I have learned that parents trust the doctor – that they talk to the doctor separately. At one time I was seriously mentally ill – my mother tried to persuade me that I needed help but I wouldn't listen. I went through several years of taking and not taking my medication and not getting the righ6 medication that would work for me. I recommend Clozaril as a good medication that works. I have learned that you will not be happy if you seek only the best in life – you need to mix the best with the ordinary. I also see another another symptom of schizophrenia – restlessly leaving a room if other are around especially if the tv is on. What I have found is that this does not happen if the tv is off and there is no other sound in the room even if there are people around. Schizophrenic people need space but at the same time people around thyem. Why does everyone pick on the mentally ill? I am feeling pretty good right now – this is my second day this way. Schizophrenic people tend to worry a lot without realising it especially about loved ones – what I have seen in the example of one of my brothers is that if you are happy the people around you will be happy.

[21] 14/01/2017

In school I developed the habit of putting on music in the. background while studying. This was making me unhappy. I did not realise that it was making me unhappy and it was affecting my concentration. Overall I am pretty happy right now though. I have my share of problems but I do not allow this to prevent me from living. Let no one tell you that you cannot have friends; a girlfriend; the right to love and the right to be forgiven if needs be. I experienced all these problems in my life AND I do not want anyone to go through what I did. An inability to say no is part of Schizophrenia whether to thoughts or other people. I realise now that other people will survive if you say no; don't worry about them

----

[22] 21/02/2017

Schizophrenia is linked to autism. I was never diagnosed as autistic – I had measles as a child something which is known to cause autism. Treating Schizophrenics as autistic may help. I was not happy in school – I did not realise I was unhappy. When being Schizophrenic I was unable to complete things that would make me happy. A negative quality of SZ is difficulty memorizing things; A positive quality is that SZ are very brave. Right now I feel stressed and unable to concentrate | I find myself fidgeting with my hands. This is my withdrawn feeling which I feel instead of being depressed. I am realising that I need rest or I will not be happy.

[23] 22/02/2017

On the few occasions I actually feel depressed I feel a need to be on my own. I especially like big rooms. The kitchen is one of the few places I feel able to be around other people. I find myself feeling depressed if I go to the cinema. I am not an adrenaline person it makes me unhappy. Being a peaceful person took a lot of suffering – I have seen this in people with manic depression. So I have a very placid nature now a lot of the time. Something to note about mentally ill patients is that they bring out the best in those who care for them. A cross I personally bear is that I cannot handle lots of noise. Another symptom of SZ is that I would turn on the radio and end up being distracted within minutes. I am unable to focus on and enjoy the music. I have found that if I keep my eyes closed though I can listen and enjoy. Try this out – praying out loud with your eyes closed. When working on something I often find myself pausing frequently and daydreaming. Sometimes I feel the need to do something, restless yet unable to focus.

[24] 23/02/2017

I think I do not need lots of medication anymore but I take it still because I know my parents would worry if I did not.

[25] 27/02/2017

I have found with SZ that I would pause and daydream repeatedly when doing homework or gardening an inability to complete things straight through. "Don't Give Up" I needed the repeated reassurance and this affirmation to keep going – when we suffer we can't see an end but the end is nearer than you think - it is sin that gets in the way. Fighting sin boosts self-esteem. This action has changed my life ever since. How do you fight sin ? Don't worry what other people think of you, your actions and your beliefs. Being honest will not always cost you. I am happier and more focused on others now. After years of suffering I have learned that I would never have made it without the help of others. I still need others help and I am now less afraid of asking others for that help. Something I learned is to be open about your illness. I did not do this growing up; I would have made far more friends if I had.

[26] 28/02/2017

I was not happy growing up in school – it took me too long to do my homework. Now I am grown up and I have options I can do online or evening courses and often at an easy pace. The courses here are more focused. I feel happy in a large room I need the space I also appreciate low noise or silence. I have also learned to do less each day and I am happier each day as a result. I like sitting near people without having to talk to them. Love is the answer to all negative relationships – active loving. I have seen that when you grow up you turn back to your parents. You do not need to wait until then to do this. There are two phrases in the bible – "Children – honour your father and mother" AND "Parents do not drive your children to resentment"

[27] 2/03/2017

I feel much happier in a large room on my own – I need the space. I also appreciate low noise or silence. I have also learned to do less each day and I am happier each day as a result. I find that when I cannot cope finding my own space to be on my own helps best. Right now I am finding it difficult to cope. Right now I depend on reassurances that I am okay and that things ARE going to work out

[28] 11/03/2017

At sixteen I had a nervous breakdown – I was schizophrenic. I had the accompanying crazy thoughts I wasn't able to say no to them – A small voice inside of me said this was wrong but I was unable to affirm these feelings. Throughout most of my life I have every so often been plagued with crazy thoughts. I would say that things do get better – but only because I have been taking medication for so long. Two things that make me feel most at peace – A walk alone in the cold night air; and crouching in front of a fire in the dark late at night. Another thing is that for a long while I have wanted to be happy before my sufferings ended. I can say now this is true.

[29] 12/03/2017

Sometimes I find it difficult to cope. I have been suffering for so long. I have become familiar with suffering. I find it hard to imagine a life without suffering.

[30] 21/03/2017

Right now I am finding it difficult to cope. I can't handle loud noise; and even being around I large numbers. I feel surrounded. What happens when you have suffered for a long time is an appreciation for the simple things

[31] 22/03/20!7

When you have suffered a lot you start to appreciate the little things in life. A walk along a forrested Lane. A breath of fresh air. Silence. Especially I have found I do not have to force this attention. My dad is like this too. I find that when things are quieter I walk more slowly and I take in more of my surrounded. I keep asking for signs a trait that many people with schizophrenia have. I have found that I am constantly telling myself things I cannot do. Crazy thinking / Worry. I have been successful in my life but experience has taught me that I cannot cope without help. What I have found is that suffering strips you of your ego and makes you more responsive to love from others.

[32] 25/03/2017

A lack of emotions is a trait of extreme schizophrenia. I am prepared to endure this cross if it helps others. A positive trait of people with SZ is that they are very brave. An affirmation I strongly recommend here is "I AM WORHY OF LOVE". Right now I feel as if my heart could break I am so devoid of emotion.

[33] 26/03/2017

At the moment it feels like my "cross" is just getting harder. It does hurt. They say "Abstinence makes the heart grow fonder". I have found that by going without food for a day; staying awake all night makes you appreciate these things even more. I have learned that every so often you have to make your own decisions without the help of others. You will make mistakes but so does everyone. I have often found the need to do a work in one go no matter how long it takes. Now I know to take breaks and spread out the work. If I cannot complete it within a certain period I just stop. I recommend taking easier school subjects in this case.

[34]:28/03/2017

Right now my faith is really weak. I've hit the limit I can take a few times. I know God goes through everything I do . I can always talk t him. Sometimes feelings don't register on the surface until they build up. Your health is your wealth so take care of yourself.